God...
Should I Be Baptized?

by Laurie Donahue
and Ralph Rittenhouse
Illustrations by Stanton Ens

LifeSong
PUBLISHERS
P.O. BOX 183 · SOMIS, CA 93066-0183
www.lifesongpublishers.com

ISBN   978-0-9718306-1-5

Published by LifeSong Publishers
P.O. Box 183, Somis, CA 93066-0183
(805) 504-3916
www.lifesongpublishers.com

All Scripture quotations taken from the *Holy Bible, New International Version®.* Copyright 1973, 1978, 1984 by International Bible Society. Used by permission of Zondervan Publishing House. All rights reserved.

Revised editions, 2005, 2011, 2014.

Illustrations by Stanton Ens
Cover art by Ed Olson

LifeSong Publishers
P.O. Box 183, Somis, CA 93066-0183
(805) 504-3916 • www.LifeSongPublishers.com
email: mailbox@LifeSongPublishers.com

God... Should I Be Baptized?

Dear Student,

I am so glad you are here, getting ready to study through this book! I know you are very important to God (because the Bible says so) and I am so glad you are making Him important in your life by taking the time to study about Him. You will learn who He is, but more than that, you will have the opportunity to have a relationship with Him.

I hope you will pay close attention to what God has to say to you as you read His Word. Then, after you have done the lesson, go back and review the previous session. Talk to your parents and family about what you are learning about God. Let God change your heart.

I am so happy to be together with you in this adventure. But, better than that, God will be with you. Throughout the next weeks, spend time talking to God. When you pray, you can ask Him to teach you what He wants you to learn, to help you understand, and to help you talk to your family about Him. Start to include Him in all areas of your life.

When you are finished with this book, I hope you will understand more of who God is and be ready for baptism. But even more, I am praying that you will have a relationship with the living God, Maker of all things, which will last forever.

Very sincerely in Him,

Laurie

Dear Parents,

We know that your child is one of the the most precious and important people in your life. As you bring, or allow him or her to come to this point of study, know that God loves them even more.

We spend time in so many areas giving our children our best. We want opportunities for them in all areas. We concentrate on sports, arts, good schools, home education, academic edge and social environment. These are all good, but do we always give the same attention to their spiritual need? Let me challenge you today to make your child's relationship with God a priority at this time. This will affect his eternity.

This book is not just about baptism, but also about the Creator of the universe and His plan for you, your child, and your family. So ask your child questions. Give him the opportunity to share with you what he is learning. Review his answers with him. And if you don't know this God already, search the Scripture for your own answers. Talk to God and seek out other believers.

While writing this book, I have prayed that I would get out of God's way and allow Him to speak directly to your child and you. I am praying for you. Dear parent, please pray for your child. Support him in his spiritual walk. These may well be the most important weeks of your child's life.

Very sincerely in Him,

Laurie

Session 1

Who's In Charge?

Discovering God's Character

Who's In Charge?

Who's in charge? God is. He created everything. Did you know that you are different from all of God's animal creatures? Animals live and breathe and eat and sleep just like you do. But you are different. Do you know why you are different?

GOD MADE YOU TO HAVE A RELATIONSHIP WITH HIM.

HE WANTS YOU TO LIVE FOREVER WITH HIM.

What Is God Like?

God... God?! Now that brings to mind a few questions. Did you know that adults have questions about God, too? Everyone has questions about God. God is so big and so different from us, we can't understand everything about Him. Even the artist who drew the above picture doesn't really know what God looks like. That is because God hasn't chosen to share EVERYTHING about Himself with us. But He has chosen to tell us some things about Himself. One of the primary ways He shares Himself is through the book He has written, the Bible. Let's look together; maybe we'll find answers to some of the questions we have.

God Is Spirit

Let's look at John 4:24.

John 4:24
God is spirit, and his worshipers must worship in spirit and in truth.

God is_____. A spirit is not a made up cartoon character or some unknown force. A spirit is a real being who thinks and makes choices, but has no body. God, the Spirit, is so big, it is hard for us to imagine.

God is Eternal

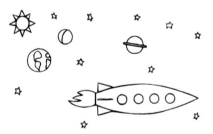

Imagine you are in a spaceship traveling through space. You pass the moon, the planets, the stars, more stars... and still more stars. Yet you don't come to the end of space. God is like that. He has no beginning and no end. It is pretty hard to imagine! Read Psalm 90:2.

Psalm 90:2
Before the mountains were born or you brought forth the earth and the world, from everlasting to everlasting you are God.

Finish writing the verse: Before the mountains were born or you brought forth the earth and the world, _____

_____

What do the words "God is eternal," mean to you now?_____

_____

God Never Changes

Did you know that God was there when you were born? God is with you now. And God will be with you when you grow old. Did you notice that the artist's picture of the man looks the same in all three pictures, and in the picture, the child changes and grows? God is like the man. Every year you change in so many ways, but God is always the same. He was the same during Bible times, the same now and will be the same at the end of time. He is the same forever. Let's read Malachi 3:6.

Malachi 3:6
I the Lord do not change.

It says, "I the Lord do _____ _____."
We change and grow but God never changes.

God Is All Powerful

Some people draw super hero cartoon characters who are strong and brave and are able to do anything. Are these characters real? Only God can do anything. Our God, Who created the world and everything that is in it, has told us in Genesis 17:1,

Genesis 17:1 "I am God Almighty."

Read Matthew 19:26.

Matthew 19:26
Jesus looked at them and said, "With man this is impossible, but with God all things are possible."

What does this verse tell us about God?_____

_____

God Knows Everything

Do you have a secret that no one else knows? Is it so secret that you have not told anyone? Not even your best friend? Did it ever occur to you that Someone has known all along?

GOD KNOWS ALL OF OUR SECRETS!

Read Psalm 139:1-4 on the next page.

Psalm 139:1-4
O Lord, you have searched me and you know me. You know when I sit and when I rise; you perceive my thoughts from afar. You discern my going out and my lying down; you are familiar with all my ways. Before a word is on my tongue you know it completely, O Lord.

Do you think you could talk to God about EVERYTHING? What does this

passage say to you? _____

_____

_____

God Is Everywhere

Has your mother or father ever said these words

to you? "You'll just have to wait. I can't be in

two places at the same time." That makes sense.

It's hard to imagine that God is everywhere. He

can be two places at once, or five... or a hundred

and five.

Jeremiah 23:24 says:

Jeremiah 23:24
Can anyone hide in secret places so that I cannot see him?" declares the Lord . "Do not I fill heaven and earth?" declares the Lord .

Do you have a secret place where you like to

hide? _____

God... Should I Be Baptized?

Think about that place. What if you turn that into a special place to meet God? What would you say to Him? What would you talk about?

_____

ANY place can be that special place. ANY time can be that special time. God is with you all the time.

God Is Faithful

Have you ever had a friend say "I'll be over this afternoon," or "I'll call you later," ...and he or she never did? Maybe you've had someone break a promise to you or maybe you have not always kept your word. Did you know that God has made over 1000 promises to us in the Bible? And He has kept every one of them.

I Corinthians 1:9 says:

> **I Corinthians 1:9**
> **God, who has called you into fellowship with his Son Jesus Christ our Lord, is faithful.**

What does this verse mean for you? _____

_____

God has promised to take care of us. On the next page are just a few verses which tell of promises God has made to you.

Can you find a promise in each verse?

1 John 1:9
If we confess our sins, he is faithful and just and will forgive us our sins and purify us from all unrighteousness.

_____

_____

Philippians 4:19
And my God will meet all your needs according to his glorious riches in Christ Jesus.

_____

_____

Romans 8:28
And we know that in all things God works for the good of those who love him, who have been called according to his purpose.

_____

_____

John 14:2
In my Father's house are many rooms; if it were not so, I would have told you. I am going there to prepare a place for you.

_____

_____

Psalm 91:14
"Because he loves me," says the Lord, "I will protect him, for he acknowledges my name."

_____

_____

God... Should I Be Baptized?

God Is Holy

Read Leviticus 19:2

Leviticus 19:2
"Speak to the entire assembly of Israel and say to them:
'Be holy because I, the Lord your God, am holy.'"

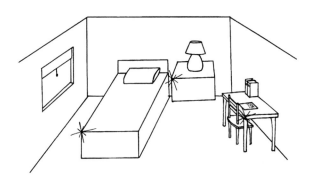

God is holy... holy? That means God is perfect. He never has and never will do anything wrong. Sinless! Not even a speck of sin on a God as big as our God!

Is your bedroom ever messy? How long does it take to clean it up? Can you even imagine a bedroom that NEVER gets messy? Not even a microscopic bit of dust on the dresser? God has no sin, like a bedroom that NEVER gets messy or dusty. It's hard to imagine, isn't it? He says, "I the Lord, your God, am _____ ." Holy means completely sinless. We can't even keep our bedroom perfectly clean, much less be perfect like God is.

God Is Fair and Just

Do you feel sometimes that things aren't fair? You

probably do, especially if you have brothers or sisters.

What do you feel is not fair? _____

We often think things are fair when they are equal.

Some things seem fair but aren't... Some things don't

seem fair but are... And some things just plain aren't

fair. But everything that God does IS fair. Read Deuteronomy 32:4.

> **Deuteronomy 32:4**
> **He is the Rock, his works are perfect, and all his ways are just. A**
> **faithful God who does no wrong, upright and just is he.**

Sometimes we think that something is fair if it is what we want. But what

is important is what God thinks. God is just, which means He is always fair

by His standard. When God asks us to be holy, and we aren't, His justice

demands a consequence. We know that He will always be fair and just... by

His rules!!

Is there a sometimes a difference between fair and just? _____

_____

God Is Love

It's hard to imagine that a God so great and powerful really cares about the

details in our lives.

God loves everything He has made. In fact, I John 4:8 tells us that

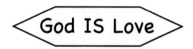

1 John 4:8
Whoever does not love does not know God, because God is love.

He wants only what is good for each of us. Read John 3:16.

John 3:16
"For God so loved the world that he gave his one and only Son, that whoever believes in him shall not perish but have eternal life.

In this verse how does God show His love? _____

_____

Today we've studied to find out what God is like. Another characteristic about God that is important for us to understand is His grace. Grace is undeserved favor. It's all the love God gives us that we haven't done anything to earn. And it's so important we'll spend our whole next session talking about how we were "lost and found."

For next week:

Memorize: I Corinthians 1:9

God, who has called you into fellowship with His Son Jesus Christ our Lord, is faithful.

Read: Genesis 1:1–31

My son/daughter has memorized the memory verse and read the Bible reading for this week.

Parent signature _____

Don't forget to review last week's session!

GETTING TO KNOW GOD BETTER

ACROSS

1. All powerful
3. God's characteristics
6. Created everything
8. One way God talks to us
9. God keeps all the _____ He makes.
12. "I the Lord do not _____."
13. "You know when I sit and when I _____."
15. God promises to meet all of our _____.
16. Perfect, sinless

DOWN

2. Knowing everything
4. Makes choices but has no body
5. God showed His love by sending _____.
6. Undeserved favor
7. How long we will live with Him as a child of God.
10. No beginning and no end
11. 1 Corinthians 1:9 says God is _____.
14. Not giving me the punishment I deserve

What Is God Like?

God has many wonderful characteristics. Solve the puzzle below to identify a few of them.

Directions: There are three or four letters on each of the file drawers. The numbers beneath the answer blanks correspond with the numbers on the drawers of the filing cabinet. Choose the file drawer that corresponds with the number on each blank. Then determine which of the letters on the file drawer you need. Write that letter in the appropriate space.

1. God is __ __ __ __ __ __. (John 4:24)
       6 5 3 5 3 6

2. God is __ __ __ __ __ __ __. (Psalm 90:2)
       2 6 2 5 4 1 4

3. God __ __ __ __ __ __ __ __ __ __ __. (Malachi 3:6)
    4 2 6 2 5   1 3 1 4 3 2 6

4. God is __ __ __ __ __ __ __ __ __ __ __. (Matthew 19:26)
      1 4 4   5 5 7 2 5 2 6 4

5. God __ __ __ __ __ __ __ __ __ __ __ __ __ __. (Psalm139:1-4)
     4 4 5 7 6   2 6 2 5 7 6 3 3 4 3

6. God is __ __ __ __ __ __ __ __ __ __. (Jeremiah 23:24)
      2 6 2 5 7 7 3 2 5 2

7. God is __ __ __ __. (Leviticus 19:2)
      3 5 4 7

8. God is __ __ __ __ __ __ __ __ __ __. (Deuteronomy 32:4)
      1 4 7 1 7 6   2 1 3 5

9. God is __ __ __ __ __ __ __ __. (1 Corinthians 1:9)
      2 1 3 6 3 2 6 4

10. God is __ __ __ __. (1 John 4:8)
      4 5 6 2

Session 2

Lost
and Found

God's Plan
for Salvation

An Awesome Beginning

Would you like to have been around when the earth was born (or at least have seen it on a video)? It must have been awesome to see something so big as our universe come out of nothing. Nothing... can you even imagine nothing? Even a dark empty closet has air in it!

Our earth is pretty big, isn't it? At least it seems so until you think about the

stars shining at night. Each star is a sun, like our sun, with planets rotating around it. And to think our eyes can see only a portion of all the stars that are up in the sky. It must be a pretty big God to be bigger than all of His creation! God's gift to us, the Bible, tells us how the world began.

God's Creation

Who was there when the world was made?

?-?-?

Read the following verses and list the three Persons who were present at the creation.

In the beginning God created the heavens and the earth. Genesis 1:1

Now the earth was formless and empty, darkness was over the surface of the deep, and the Spirit of God was hovering over the waters. Genesis 1:2

In the beginning was the Word, and the Word was with God, and the Word was God. He was with God in the beginning. The Word became flesh and made his dwelling among us. We have seen his glory, the glory of the One and Only, who came from the Father, full of grace and truth. John 1:1-2 & 14

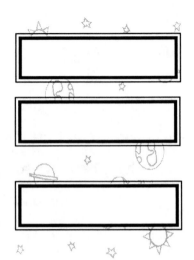

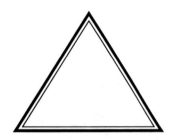

Think of a triangle. It has three sides. It is not a triangle if a side is missing, yet with all sides, it is one triangle. God is like that— three Persons yet only one God. This is one of God's mysteries.

You can read the rest of the exciting creation story in Genesis 1 and 2.

How did God feel about all the things He had created?

Genesis 1:31
God saw all that he had made, and it was very good. And there was evening, and there was morning—the sixth day.

_____

_____

_____

_____

_____

28   God... Should I Be Baptized?

Look up Genesis 1:26. Who were people like when they were created? In what ways were they like Him? _____

_____

God's Perfect Creation Was Ruined

In Genesis 2, compare what God told Adam and Eve about the tree of the knowledge of good and evil with what the serpent told them about the tree in the following verses.

Genesis 2:15-17
The Lord God took the man and put him in the Garden of Eden to work it and take care of it. And the Lord God commanded the man, "You are free to eat from any tree in the garden; but you must not eat from the tree of the knowledge of good and evil, for when you eat of it you will surely die."

Genesis 3:1-5
Now the serpent was more crafty than any of the wild animals the Lord God had made. He said to the woman, "Did God really say, 'You must not eat from any tree in the garden'?" The woman said to the serpent, "We may eat fruit from the trees in the garden, but God did say, 'You must not eat fruit from the tree that is in the middle of the garden, and you must not touch it, or you will die.'" "You will not surely die," the serpent said to the woman. "For God knows that when you eat of it your eyes will be opened, and you will be like God, knowing good and evil."

What God Said	What the Serpent Said

What would you have done if you were in their situation?

_____

_____

Why or why not?

_____

_____

_____

Read Genesis 3:6.

Genesis 3:6
When the woman saw that the fruit of the tree was good for food and pleasing to the eye, and also desirable for gaining wisdom, she took some and ate it. She also gave some to her husband, who was with her, and he ate it.

Did Adam and Eve obey or disobey God? _____

What two things entered the world because of their disobedience?

Romans 5:12
Therefore, just as sin entered the world through one man, and death through sin, and in this way death came to all men, because all sinned—

_____ and _____

How does Adam and Eve's sin affect you and me?_____

_____

_____

According to Romans 3:23, how many people have sinned?

Romans 3:23
...for all have sinned and fall short of the glory of God,

_____

God... Should I Be Baptized?

What Is Sin?

God told them if they ate from the tree of the knowledge of good and evil, they would die. And they chose to disobey. That choice resulted in a LOSS

OF FELLOWSHIP WITH GOD for all mankind. Later, He gave a list of laws He wanted all people to obey. Some of them are listed in Exodus 20:1-17. Can you find ten? You can circle those you find.

And God spoke all these words:

"I am the Lord your God, who brought you out of Egypt, out of the land of slavery. You shall have no other gods before me. You shall not make for yourself an idol in the form of anything in heaven above or on the earth beneath or in the waters below. You shall not bow down to them or worship them; for I, the Lord your God, am a jealous God, punishing the children for the sin of the fathers to the third and fourth generation of those who hate me, but showing love to a thousand ⟨generations⟩ of those who love me and keep my commandments.

You shall not misuse the name of the Lord your God, for the Lord will not hold anyone guiltless who misuses his name. Remember the Sabbath day by keeping it holy. Six days you shall labor and do all your work, but the seventh day is a Sabbath to the Lord your God. On it you shall not do any work, neither you, nor your son or daughter, nor your manservant or maidservant, nor your animals, nor the alien within your gates. For in six days the Lord made the heavens and the earth, the sea, and all that is in them, but he rested on the seventh day. Therefore the Lord blessed the Sabbath day and made it holy. Honor your father and your mother, so that you may live long in the land the Lord your God is giving you. You shall not murder. You shall not commit adultery. You shall not steal. You shall not give false testimony against your neighbor. You shall not covet your neighbor's house. You shall not covet your neighbor's wife, or his manservant or maidservant, his ox or donkey, or anything that belongs to your neighbor."

1. Love God

2. God First

3. Speak Purely

4. Give God His Day

5. Honor Mom & Dad

6. Don't Murder

7. Be Faithful

8. Don't Steal

9. Be Truthful

10. Be Content

Sin is not obeying God.

Read James 2:10.

James 2:10
For whoever keeps the whole law and yet stumbles at just one point is guilty of breaking all of it.

What does it say to you about your sin? _____

_____

What is the result of sin in our lives according to Romans 6:23?

Romans 6:23
For the wages of sin is death, but the gift of God is eternal life in Christ Jesus our Lord.

_____

God... Should I Be Baptized?

What kind of death is this verse talking about? _____

_____

But God doesn't leave us like this! For encouragement, READ ON!

God's Solution

Even though we have all sinned and should be separated from God forever,

God still loves us and has provided a way for us to be forgiven.

Read Acts 13:38.

> **Acts 13:38**
> "Therefore, my brothers, I want you to know that through Jesus the forgiveness of sins is proclaimed to you.

Through Whom do we have forgiveness?

_____

Who was Jesus? Read John 14:6.

> **John 14:6**
> Jesus answered, "I am the way and the truth and the life. No one comes to the Father except through me."

_____

What did He do?

> **1 Corinthians 15:3-4**
> For what I received I passed on to you as of first importance: that Christ died for our sins according to the Scriptures, that he was buried, that he was raised on the third day according to the Scriptures,

_____

_____

Christ paid the penalty for our sins. He met God's requirement in place of us.

Read the following verses and tell what a person needs to do to receive the

free gift of eternal life.

John 1:12
Yet to all who received him, to those who believed in his name, he gave the right to become children of God—

John 3:16
For God so loved the world that he gave his one and only Son, that whoever believes in him shall not perish but have eternal life.

_____

What else is part of believing and receiving? Read the following verses.

1 John 1:9
If we confess our sins, he is faithful and just and will forgive us our sins and purify us from all unrighteousness.

Mark 1:15
"The time has come," he said. "The kingdom of God is near. Repent and believe the good news!"

_____

To confess our sins means to "agree with God about our sins." To repent

means to "turn away from our sins, toward God." How can YOU have

this forgiveness? _____

Do you believe that Jesus Christ is the Son of God and died to pay

for your sins? _____ Are you ready to turn from your

sin and let Him be in charge of your life? _____

Would you like to pray right now and thank Him for dying

for you and forgiving you?

God... Should I Be Baptized?

If you don't know the right words to use, you can say this prayer:

> *Dear God,*
> *Thank you for loving me so much that you sent Jesus, Your Son, to die for me. I am sorry for all of the times I have not obeyed You. I am placing complete trust in what Jesus did on the cross to pay for my sins. I want to obey You. I want You to be the Lord of my life. I thank You that You forgive me and I will live forever with You because of what Jesus has done.*
> *AMEN*

Did you know that when you ask Jesus to be your Savior and Lord He makes a promise to you? What is that promise?

Hebrews 13:5
"Never will I leave you; never will I forsake you."

_____

How long will He be your Savior and Friend?

_____

For next week:

Memorize: I John 1:9

If we confess our sins, he is faithful and just and will forgive us

our sins and purify us from all unrighteousness.

Read: Acts 8:26-40

My son/daughter has memorized the memory verse and read the

Bible reading for this week.

Parent signature _____

Don't forget to review last week's session!

God... Should I Be Baptized?

And Jesus Did It For Me?

ACROSS

4. Became flesh and dwelt among us
7. Sin resulted in loss of _____ with God
8. Number of Persons that are part of God
10. Christ paid this for our sin
13. Jesus was ____ on the third day according to the Scriptures
14. God's _____ caused Him to send Jesus to us
16. God will never _____ or forsake us

DOWN

1. What God did on the seventh day
2. Length of time Jesus will be our Savior and Friend
3. When Adam and Eve ate of the fruit they _____ God
5. Hovered over the waters before the earth was created
6. World was created in _____ days
9. What we deserve because of our sin, what entered the world because of sin
11. Eternal life is a ___ gift to us
12. Tells us how the world began
15. Number of sins required to be guilty of all sin

God... Should I Be Baptized?

If there had been a daily newspaper in Bible times, it may have published articles like the one below. Use the alphabet code to fill in the missing words from the articles.

Trinity Times

Published Daily   **Issue 1- Bible Times**

A Beautiful Beginning

In the last seven days, many changes have taken place in the __ __ __ __ __.
                                                    23 15 18 12 4

What was once __ __ __ __ and __ __ __ __ is now alive with __ __ __ __ __,
                      4 1 18 11   3 15 12 4   3 15 12 15 18

sights and sounds. This kind of __ __ __ __ __ __ __ __ __ handi-work could only
                                  3 18 5 1 20 9 22 5

be accomplished by __ __ __. Sources from the book of Genesis have been
                        7 15 4

quoted as saying, "God saw all He __ __ __ __ and it was __ __ __ __!"
                                  13 1 4 5   7 15 15 4

Perfect Creation Ruined

It has been reported that __ __ __, the product of the sixth day of
                            13 1 14

__ __ __ __ __ __ __ __, failed to keep the __ __ __ __ God gave him. When
3 18 5 1 20 9 15 14   18 21 12 5

placed in the beautiful __ __ __ __ __ __, he was instructed not to eat the
                         7 1 18 4 5 14

__ __ __ __ __ from the __ __ __ __ of the knowledge of good and evil. He chose to listen
6 18 21 9 20   20 18 5 5

to a serpent and this act of __ __ __ __ __ __ __ __ __ __ __ __ has resulted in
                          4 9 19 15 2 5 4 9 5 14 3 4

__ __ __. God told man that if he sinned, he must __ __ __. Throughout time man
19 9 14   4 9 5

continues to sin. Sin __ __ __ __ __ __ __ __ __ __ us from God.
                 19 5 16 1 18 1 20 5 19

Good News!

In a recent turn of events, the problem of man having

to die for his __ __ __ *has been solved. Because of God's*
                          19 9 14

__ __ __ __ *for us He provided a* __ __ __ __.
12 15 22 5   16 12 1 14

God sent His __ __ __, __ __ __ __ __ __ *to pay the penalty*
                  19 15 14 10 5 19 21 19

for us. Because of his death on the cross, we can __ __ __ __ __ __ __
                                      3 15 14 6 5 19 19

our sin to God and have __ __ __ __ __ __ __ __ __ __ __.
                      6 15 18 7 9 22 5 14 5 19 19

This is __ __ __ __ __ __ __ __ *for all!*
         7 15 15 4 14 5 23 19

Alphabet Code

A	B	C	D	E	F	G	H	I
1	2	3	4	5	6	7	8	9
J	K	L	M	N	O	P	Q	R
1O	11	12	13	14	15	16	17	18
S	T	U	V	W	X	Y	Z	
19	20	21	22	23	24	25	26	

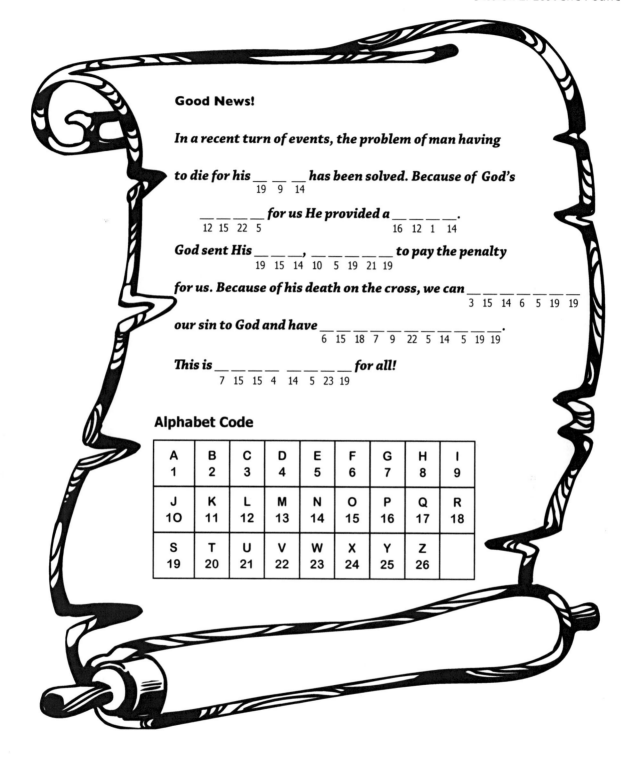

God... Should I Be Baptized?

Session 3

Baptism...
Is it for Me?

Why, What, When
Where How?

Pretty Dirty?

"Wow, do you need a bath. You must be somewhere under all that dirt."

Has anyone ever said something like that to
you? After playing outside all day, we can
get pretty dirty. A bath or shower can do
wonders for the way we look. A little clean
up and you may even look like a new person.

But no matter how long you soak, or rub, or scrub, it won't do anything about
the mud on the inside. Isaiah 64:6 describes what we look like on the inside
before we are washed.

> **Isaiah 64:6**
> **All of us have become like one who is unclean, and all our righteous acts are like
> filthy rags; we all shrivel up like a leaf, and like the wind our sins sweep us away.**

Sounds pretty bad, doesn't it? Last lesson we talked about the one and only
one way we can get cleaned up on the inside.

> **1 John 1:9**
> **If we confess our sins, he is faithful and just and will forgive us our sins and purify
> us from all unrighteousness.**

Are you clean on the inside? _____ Why?_____

_____

What did you do or say? _____

_____

_____

The thought of our God forgiving ALL of our sins is pretty amazing. How do you respond to a God who would care about you that much?

John 14:15
"If you love me, you will obey what I command. "

_____

One of Jesus' greatest commands is found in Matthew 28:19.

Therefore go and make disciples of all nations, baptizing them in the name of the Father and of the Son and of the Holy Spirit,...

What does He command us to do? _____

_____

Baptism

Baptism. That's an interesting word. If you look in a Greek dictionary, you might find a similar word. The word "Baptizo" in Greek means "to dip" or "to wash." But we already said there is one and only one way to be washed on the inside.

John 15:3
You are already clean because of the word I have spoken to you.

Jesus says that way is _____

_____

So we are actually washed of our sin before baptism.

Baptism Is A Symbol

Baptism is a symbol of three things.

❶ Baptism is a symbol of our washing. When your sports team wins the championship, you get a trophy. The trophy isn't the team or the game or even the winning moment, but a symbol of the great playing that happened all season. Baptism is the symbol, or picture, of the washing that has taken place inside of us when we have confessed our sin and we receive Christ as our Lord and Savior.

❷ It is also a symbol of Jesus' death and resurrection.

Read Romans 6:3-5.

> **Romans 6:3-5**
> Or don't you know that all of us who were baptized into Christ Jesus were baptized into his death? We were therefore buried with him through baptism into death in order that, just as Christ was raised from the dead through the glory of the Father, we too may live a new life. If we have been united with him like this in his death, we will certainly also be united with him in his resurrection.

From these verses, can you compare each of the following parts of baptism to the part of Christ's death and resurrection it symbolizes?

Baptism	Christ's Death and Resurrection
Going Under the Water	
Coming Out of the Water	

❸ Baptism symbolizes a third truth. We are part His body of believers.

Read I Corinthians 12:13 and Colossians 1:18.

> **1 Corinthians 12:13**
> **For we were all baptized by one Spirit into one body—whether Jews or Greeks, slave or free—and we were all given the one Spirit to drink.**
>
> **Colossians 1:18a**
> **And he is the head of the body, the church.**

"For we were all baptized by one Spirit into one _____ -whether

Jews or Greeks, slaves or free- and we were all given the one Spirit to drink."

The body is _____.

Now let's look back at what we just talked about. Can you list the three

truths that baptism symbolizes?

1. _____

_____

2. _____

_____

3. _____

_____

Why Should We Be Baptized?

So why should we be baptized? (Remember Matthew 28:19?) _____

_____

Yes! Because God told us to. It is important to follow Jesus' example.

Read about His baptism in Mark 1:9-11.

Mark 1:9-11
At that time Jesus came from Nazareth in Galilee and was baptized by John in the Jordan. As Jesus was coming up out of the water, he saw heaven being torn open and the Spirit descending on him like a dove. And a voice came from heaven: "You are my Son, whom I love; with you I am well pleased."

Maybe you've watched or played a baseball game. Each

player has his own uniform so you know exactly which

team he is on. Also, each player has his own number

so you can identify exactly who he is. Read Matthew 10:32.

Matthew 10:32
"Whoever acknowledges me before men, I will also acknowledge him before my Father in heaven.

Can you tell another reason for baptism? _____

_____

Who Should Be Baptized?

Who should be baptized? In Acts 2:41 the Apostle Peter was

talking to a large group of people. Read Acts 2:41.

Acts 2:41
Those who accepted his message were baptized, and about three thousand were added to their number that day.

Some were baptized and some were not. Which were baptized?

_____

God... Should I Be Baptized?

What the Bible Says About Baptism

In Acts 8:12 we are told of two more baptisms. In these verses what two things did the men and women do?

Acts 8:12
But when they believed Philip as he preached the good news of the kingdom of God and the name of Jesus Christ, they were baptized, both men and women.

1. _____

2. _____

What must YOU do before you are baptized? _____

_____

In our homework this week we read a detailed story of an Ethiopian official in Acts 8:26-40. It's fun to have a peek at how someone else came to Christ many years ago. How long did the Ethiopian official wait before he was baptized? _____

_____

From Acts, 8:38-39 describe how we are to be baptized.

_____

Should You Be Baptized?

Would you like to be baptized?

Have you:

❏ Asked Jesus to be your Lord and Savior?

❏ Asked for forgiveness, been truly sorry, and turned from sin?

❏ Decided you want to obey and follow Him?

❏ Decided you want to be baptized?

If you could check these boxes... then YES! Be baptized!

Can you describe when, where and how you received Christ as your Lord and Savior?

If you want to be baptized, fill out the following:

I, _____ would like to be baptized. I am sorry for my sin and have accepted Jesus Christ as my Lord and Savior. I want to obey His command and follow Him.

Signed: _____

Date: _____

Parent Signature: _____

For next week:

Memorize:
Matthew 28:19-20.

Therefore go and make disciples of all nations, baptizing them in the name of the Father and of the Son and of the Holy Spirit, and teaching them to obey everything I have commanded you. And surely I am with you always, to the very end of the age.

Read: I John 2:3-6 and Ephesians 3:20

My son/daughter has memorized the memory verse and read the Bible reading for this week.

Parent Signature _____

Don't forget to review last week's session!

God... Should I Be Baptized?

What Is Baptism, Again?

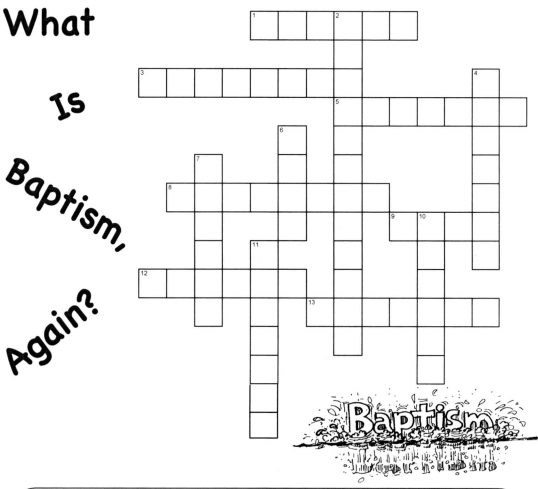

ACROSS

1. Body of believers
3. One reason we are baptized is because He _____ us to
5. What we have become like in Isaiah 64:6
8. In Acts 8:12, people were baptized after they _____
9. The man who baptized Jesus
12. River where Jesus was baptized
13. In 1 John 1:9, it says we must _____ our sins

DOWN

2. Baptism symbolizes Christ's death and _____
4. Baptism symbolizes our inside _____
6. If we love God, we will _____ His commands
7. Are we washed of our sin before or after baptism?
10. When we are baptized, we show _____ what we believe
11. Means to dip or to wash

Who Should Be Baptized?

To answer the question of "who should be baptized?" you will need to find your way through the maze of letters. Begin in the upper left-hand corner marked "start." Follow each set of directions until you come to the word *stop*. Then write that letter in a blank below. When you finish you will have the answer that you can also find by following God's directions in His Word!

1. Go 1 space to the right, then down 1 space, *stop.*

2. Go down 2 spaces, move 2 spaces to the right, and up 1, *stop.*

3. Go 2 spaces to the right, *stop.*

4. Go down 3 spaces, *stop.*

5. Go 1 space to the left, then go up 4 spaces, *stop.*

6. Go 2 spaces to the left, then down 5 spaces, *stop.*

7. Go 2 spaces to the right, then down 1 space, *stop.*

8. Go down 2 spaces, *stop.*

9. Go up 1 space, then to the right 3 spaces, *stop.*

10. Go up 2 spaces, move 1 space to the left, *stop.*

11. Go 2 spaces to the left, then up 2 spaces, *stop.*

12. Go up 2 spaces, to the left 2 spaces and down 2 spaces, *stop.*

13. Go down 5 spaces, *stop.*

14. Go 4 spaces to the right, move 6 spaces up, *stop.*

15. Go 5 spaces to the left and down 2 spaces, *stop.*

16. Go down 3 spaces, then go 2 spaces to the right, *stop.*

17. Go up 1 space, *stop.*

18. Go up 7 spaces, *stop.*

19. Go 4 spaces to the right, Go down 4 spaces, *stop.*

20. Go down 3 spaces, then 7 spaces to the left, *stop.*

21. Go up 4 spaces, Go 1 space to the right, *stop.*

22. Go to the left 1 space, then up 2 spaces, *stop.*

23. Go 8 spaces to the right, move down 2, *stop.*

24. Go 8 spaces to the left, then up 1 space, stop.

25. Go 7 spaces to the right, stop.

God... Should I Be Baptized?

____ _ ____ ____ ____ ____   ____ ____ ____

____ ____ ____ ____ ____ ____ ____

____ _ ____ ____

____ ____ ____ ____ ____ ____ ____ .

(Hint: See Acts 8:12)

Start	R	C	D	T	O	N	L	C
E	T	B	U	E	B	D	F	M
V	U	L	H	S	O	T	E	Q
O	C	F	G	H	V	V	J	I
K	W	I	Y	L	N	C	R	M
H	E	L	P	X	S	B	L	T
D	G	W	K	U	A	E	P	W
E	B	S	N	H	L	Y	C	N
R	L	T	A	J	I	P	B	C
F	B	E	T	O	W	M	D	H

Session 4

Following God's Game Plan

Doing What God Wants Me To Do

Playing According to God's Game Plan

We've sure learned a lot about God in the last few sessions! We've learned why we can trust God to do exactly what He says He will do. We've learned about our free gift of salvation through Jesus Christ. And we've learned about the baptism to which He calls us. Pretty exciting, isn't it?

Now picture yourself playing on a team. It could be any type of team, but

let's pretend it's a baseball team. Would you ever think of taking your homework out to third base or writing a letter between pitches if you were a pitcher? If you were a gymnast, would you practice a swim stroke on the parallel bars? Would you try to shoot a basket

in a soccer game? Once you have committed yourself to a sport or team, you would follow the rules of the game and be the best player you could be, even when you don't feel like it. You would follow the game plan for the sport you are playing.

God has a game plan for Christians, too!

God Wants Us to Obey

1 John 2:3-6
We know that we have come to know him if we obey his commands. The man who says, "I know him", but does not do what he commands is a liar, and the truth is not in him. But if anyone obeys his word, God's love is truly made complete in him. This is how we know we are in him: Whoever claims to live in him must walk as Jesus did.

Fill in the missing words. "But if anyone _____ His word, God's _____ is truly made complete in him." Would you like to have God's love be complete in you? _____

Read Romans 12:1

Romans 12:1
Therefore, I urge you, brothers, in view of God's mercy, to offer your bodies as living sacrifices, holy and pleasing to God—this is your spiritual act of worship.

What is this verse telling us to be? _____

What is a sacrifice? _____

What is a living sacrifice? _____

What can you do to be a living sacrifice? _____

_____

Read Romans 6:13.

> **Romans 6:13**
> Do not offer the parts of your body to sin, as instruments of wickedness, but rather offer yourselves to God, as those who have been brought from death to life; and offer the parts of your body to him as instruments of righteousness.

What is this verse telling us to be? _____

What is an instrument? _____

How can you be an instrument of God's righteousness? _____

God Gives Us His Power

Can you think of a favorite battery operated toy you have had in the past? Think of the energy the toy had with new batteries. Do you remember a time when the batteries began to run down? Did the toy slow down, become dimmer or just quit working? Have your headphones ever become disconnected to your media player while you were listening? God is not like that. God NEVER runs out of power! He gives us His power to be what He wants us to be—and the supply never runs out!

> **Ephesians 3:20**
> Now to him who is able to do immeasurably more than all we ask or imagine, according to his power that is at work within us...

According to Ephesians 3:20, Who is able to do immeasurably more than we ask or imagine? _____ What is at work within us? _____

God Wants Us to Pray

Look up Philippians 4:6-7 and fill in the missing words. "Do not be anxious about anything, but in everything, by prayer and petition, with _____, present your requests to God. And the _____ of God, which transcends all understanding, will guard your hearts and your minds in _____ _____."

Instead of being anxious, we are to _____. How many things does God want us to pray about? _____.

Our prayers should include petition and _____.

What will guard your heart and mind? _____.

In Whom can we find peace? _____.

From 1 Thessalonians 5:16-18 list three ways we should pray.

1 Thessalonians 5:16-18
Be joyful always; pray continually; give thanks in all circumstances, for this is God's will for you in Christ Jesus.

1. _____

2. _____

3. _____

God Wants Us To Study His Word

In the first session we talked about how God shows Himself to us. In

2 Timothy 3:15-16 He tells us about one way He talks to us.

> **2 Timothy 3:15-16**
> ...and how from infancy you have known the holy Scriptures, which are able to make you wise for salvation through faith in Christ Jesus. All Scripture is God-breathed and is useful for teaching, rebuking, correcting and training in righteousness...

What is that way? _____

Can you find four things for which Scripture is useful?

1. _____

2. _____

3. _____

4. _____

> **2 Timothy 3:17**
> ...so that the man of God may be thoroughly equipped for every good work.

Can you find a fifth thing in verse 17?

5. _____

In Joshua 1:8 God gives us instruction for meditation.

> **In Joshua 1:8**
> Do not let this Book of the Law depart from your mouth; meditate on it day and night, so that you may be careful to do everything written in it. Then you will be prosperous and successful.

What does it mean to meditate? _____

What will be the result of meditating on His law? _____

_____

God Wants Us To Go To Church

Sports teams have pep talks and rallies to encourage their members. There is strong commitment between individuals to help each other do their best. Christ put His church on earth for that same reason. We are to support and encourage one another in our walk with the Lord. Hebrews 10:24-25 tells us why we should meet together.

> **Hebrews 10:24-25**
> **And let us consider how we may spur one another on toward love and good deeds. Let us not give up meeting together, as some are in the habit of doing, but let us encourage one another—and all the more as you see the Day approaching.**

Toward what two things should we spur on one another?

1._____ 2._____ _____

Acts 2:42 describes what the believers in the early church did when they came together.

> **Acts 2:42**
> **They devoted themselves to the apostles' teaching and to the fellowship, to the breaking of bread and to prayer.**

Can you find four things they did?

1._____

2._____

3._____

4._____

What is your favorite part of church?

_____

God Wants Us To
Tell Others About Jesus

Now that you have met Jesus, do you think your friends would like to know

Him, too? Read John 1:41.

John 1:41
**The first thing Andrew did was to find his brother Simon and tell him, "We
have found the Messiah" (that is, the Christ).**

What is the first thing Andrew did after he found Jesus? _____

_____

What did he say?_____

Read 1 Peter 3:15.

1 Peter 3:15
**But in your hearts set apart Christ as Lord.
Always be prepared to give an answer to
everyone who asks you to give the reason
for the hope that you have. But do this
with gentleness and respect.**

God... Should I Be Baptized?

If someone asks you about the hope you have, what should you be prepared

to do? _____

Romans 1:16
I am not ashamed of the gospel, because it is the power of God for the salvation of everyone who believes: first for the Jew, then for the Gentile.

In Romans 1:16, Paul said he was not ashamed of the gospel because it is

the _____ of God for the _____ of

everyone who _____. Can you list the names of several

people you could talk to about Jesus this week? _____

_____

Does all of this sound like a pretty tough assignment? A good verse to think

about is Philippians 4:13. Let's say it together:

Philippians 4:13
"I can do everything through him who gives me strength."

Try to think of this verse three times a day every day this week. Where does

your strength come from to do what God wants you to do? _____

_____

PLAY IT BY THE BOOK

Keeping God's rules will make us happier people.

Read Psalm 119:14.

Psalm 119:14
I rejoice in following your statutes as one rejoices in great riches.

Describe what a result will be for you if you follow God's commands.

_____

God... Should I Be Baptized?

Read Ezekiel 36:26-27 and look for two things God has given to you to help you follow His commands.

Ezekiel 36:26-27
I will give you a new heart and put a new spirit in you; I will remove from you your heart of stone and give you a heart of flesh. And I will put my Spirit in you and move you to follow my decrees and be careful to keep my laws.

1._____

2_____

Are you running bases in a football game or are you with the game plan? Are you carefully thinking about what God has asked you to do and following His rules? Are there any new things you have learned today that you will want to do since you are on God's team? What are they? _____

_____

_____

Let's take a moment to pray about our walk with Christ, Who has provided your salvation through

faith in Him...

For next week:

No new homework this week.

But don't forget to review all of the sessions!!!

I Really Want to Obey God!

ACROSS

1. We obey God's _____
5. God gives us this so we can do what he asks
10. One thing for which Scripture is useful
11. Acts 2:42 describes _____ things the believers did together
12. To tell others what you have seen or know to be true
13. God's _____ which guards our hearts and minds
14. We should encourage each other in good _____
15. Our prayers should include petition and _____

DOWN

2. To do what we are asked
3. Giving up of something costly
4. We offer our bodies as _____ sacrifices
6. How we should pray
7. A tool used to accomplish a purpose
8. God talks to us through the _____
9. To study and think about

Part Of The Team!

When we are part of God's team, there are some things God wants us to do. Use the secret morse code below to detect six of them. Look up the code and put the correct letter on the line above.

1.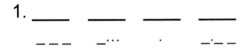

2.

3.

4.

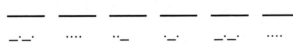

5.

God... Should I Be Baptized?

Puzzle (top):

_____ _____ _____ _____ _____
.-   -... ---   .-.   -

_____ _____ _____ _____ _____ _____
---   -   ....   .   .-.   ...

_____ _____ _____ _____ _____ !
.--- --   .-   .-.   ...

6. _____ _____ _____ _____ _____ _____ _____ _____ _____ _____
    ...   .   .-.   ..-   .   .---   .   ...   ..-   ...

_____ _____ _____ _____ _____ _____ _____ _____ _____ _____
.-   ...   .-.   --   .-   -.   ---   .-.

_____ _____ _____ _____ _____ _____ _____ _____ !
-.-- ---   .-   .-   -.-   ..   .-.

Morse Code

A ._	H	O _ _ _	V ..._
B _...	I ..	P ._ _.	W ._ _
C _._.	J ._ _ _	Q _ _._	X _.._
D _..	K _._	R ._.	Y _._ _
E .	L ._..	S ...	Z _ _..
F .._.	M _ _	T _	
G _ _.	N _.	U .._	

Review and Beyond
Session 1

1. In what way are people different from the rest of the world that God created?

2. How does God show Himself to us?

3. The Bible tells us that God is Spirit. What does that mean?

4. We usually think of eternal as having no end. What is another aspect of eternal?

5. How can the God that the Old Testament Jews worshiped and our God be the same?

6. If God can help you do anything in your life, why doesn't He?

God... Should I Be Baptized?

7. If God already knows your sinful thoughts, why do you try to hide them from Him?

8. What can you do to establish a regular time to meet with God?

9. How can you ever be as holy as God expects?

10. What is a difference between "fair" and "just"? Which best describes God?

11. When we say that God is faithful, what does it mean? How does it affect your faith?

12. Is grace more than the prayer before a meal? What is it?

Review and Beyond
Session 2

1. What three Persons were present at the earth's creation?

2. We worship three Persons... Do we worship three gods? Explain!

3. What does it mean to be created in God's image? Are we still in His image?

4. If Adam and Eve were perfect, why did they sin?

5. What two things entered the world because of Adam and Eve's disobedience?

6. Is it ever possible for you to "not sin"? If yes, then when? If not, then why try?

God... Should I Be Baptized?

7. Define "sin."

8. What can you see are some of the results of sin in the world?

9. What is the result of sin in your life? How does it affect you physically and spiritually?

10. What is God's solution for sin? How does it involve you?

11. What does a person need to do to receive eternal life?

12. What is the difference between "confess" and "repent"? How do they relate to each other?

13. What does it mean to ask Jesus to be Lord of your life?

Review and Beyond
Session 3

1. How is it possible to stand before God with a clean heart and clean thoughts?

2. Is there any sin that God will not forgive? What would it be?

3. What command does Jesus give His followers in Matthew 28:19?

4. Does baptism remove your sin? Explain.

5. What are three things that baptism symbolizes?

    1.

    2.

    3.

God... Should I Be Baptized?

6. What does rising out of the water in baptism represent?

7. Can you list three reasons a person should be baptized?

8. How does baptism make a statement to all those who see?

9. What must a person do before they are baptized?

10. Is there ever a case when a person should not be baptized?

11. Why do you think God commanded baptism?

12. If sin is not removed through baptism, how might baptism change you?

Review and Beyond
Session 4

1. What are several reasons to obey God?

2. Compare the Old Testament sacrifice to the New Testament sacrifice described in Romans.

3. Why might God not give you something you asked Him for?

4. If you think God is telling you something, how do you know if it is really God speaking to you?

5. Can you list five things for which Scripture is useful?

6. What are some ways others in your church can help and support you?

God... Should I Be Baptized?

7. What can you do to support others in their walk with the Lord?

8. Why is it a good idea to write out your testimony?

9. Where does your strength come from to do a difficult task?

10. Will God give you the strength to do something that is not in His will?

11. Why is it important to remain very close to God through prayer, fellowship, and reading His Word?

12. Now that you have the rest of your life ahead of you... how will it be different?

Making Sense of Terms

It can be confusing when people in different churches, or even people in the same church, use a different term than you have learned for the same thing. There are several terms for "received the gift of salvation through Jesus." Look at the terms below. They mean basically the same thing, so when you hear them you will recognize them as what you have heard before.

Been Saved

Accepted Christ

Become a Christian

Asked Jesus into Your Heart

Are a Believer

Know the Lord

Been Born Again

Given Your Life To Jesus

Been Redeemed

Have The Gift of Eternal life

God... Should I Be Baptized?

Types Of Questions My Pastor May Ask Me
Before I Am Baptized

1. Why do you want to be baptized?

2. How do you know that you are going to heaven?

3. When did you receive Jesus Christ as Savior?

4. What does baptism mean or show?

5. What will happen at your baptism?

6. After baptism, what will you do to show that you are on God's team and He is Ruler of your life?

7. Are you wanting to be baptized to please someone else or is this something you really want to do?

When You Are Baptized

You may want to bring:

Complete change of dry clothes
towel
comb or brush
hair dryer
plastic sack for wet clothes
camera

We were therefore buried with him through baptism into death in order that, just as Christ was raised from the dead through the glory of the Father, we too may live a new life.
Romans 6:4

Encourage a family member or friend to take a picture and/or video during the baptism so you have a visual remembrance of this momentous day.

Remember:

You are obeying God and have His total support. The congregation supports you in your decision as well.

PHOTOS....

God... Should I Be Baptized?

NOTES OF ENCOURAGEMENT

What I Remember Best About My Baptism Day

_____

_____

_____

_____

_____

_____

_____

_____

_____

_____

_____

_____

_____

_____

_____

_____

_____

This page and the following page may be photocopied on special paper

God... Should I Be Baptized?

CERTIFICATE OF BAPTISM

In keeping with the Bible's Commandment

has chosen to follow Christ in baptism and was baptized in the name of the Father, and of the Son, and of the Holy Spirit

on the _____ day of _____ ,

in the year of our Lord _____ .

"Go ye therefore and teach all nations, baptizing them in the name of the Father and of the Son and of the Holy Spirit."
Matthew 28:19

_____
Pastor

Glossary

Amen- so it is, or so it shall be

Apostle- one who Christ Himself chose to preach the gospel

Atonement- the restoration of relationship between God and man made possible by Jesus' death and resurrection

Blemish- a mark or area of imperfection

Carnal- worldly, sinful, corrupt

Christ- Messiah, Anointed One

Christian- one who believes in Jesus Christ as eternal Son of God and trusts in Him only for salvation

Communion- fellowship, the sharing of thoughts or feelings

Condemnation- punishment for sin, severe reproof

Confession- agreeing with God concerning our sin, admitting guilt

Conversion- God's act of working faith in Christ Jesus in the heart of one who does not believe

Corruptible- susceptible to depravation, subject to decay

Death- *Physical death*: of the body
Spiritual death: separation from God through our refusal to trust in Jesus Christ
Eternal death: separation from God forever

Doctrine- a teaching

Eternal- has no beginning or no end

Evangelical- pertaining to the Gospel or the spreading of the Gospel

Exhort- to urge to do what is right

Everlasting- goes on forever

Faith- trust and reliance in that which you cannot see but are confident

Fall of Man (the fall)- refers to the first act of disobedience by Adam and Eve in the Garden of Eden

Fear of God- appropriate respect and honor of God.

Flesh- man's sinful nature, his inability to do what God commands

Gentile- a non-Jew

Glorify- to worship, give glory, honor or high praise to, exalt

Good works- those things we do which we perceive as worthy

Gospel- good news of Jesus Christ

Grace- undeserved love or favor

Holy- pure, sinless

Hypocrite- one who pretends to be something he is not

Immersion- immersing or dipping

Immutable- unchangeable, unalterable

Incarnate- God, the Son, became man in the form of Jesus Christ, while retaining His divine nature

Iniquity- sin, depravation

Intercession- pleading on behalf of others

Judgment- punishment, a just decision

Just- lawful, right, righteous, guiltless

Justification- God declares a sinner righteous, "just as if I had never sinned"

Kingdom- sphere in which a king has sovereign control

Law- commandments from God, sometimes refers to "the Word the Bible"

Meditate- Keep it in your mind, constantly think about something

Mercy- not giving me the punishment I deserve

Mortal- subject to death

Omnipotent- all powerful

Omnipresent-can be everywhere at one time

Omniscience- knows everything, all-knowing

Perish- to die or be destroyed

Petition- a solemn request to a superior authority

God... Should I Be Baptized?

Prayer- conversation with God

Predestination- being predetermined

Prophecy- making God's will known to people

Purify- to cleanse, remove impurities, free from sin and guilt

Redeem, Redemption- to buy back, Jesus Christ bought us back from sin and death with His death and resurrection

Remission- forgiveness

Repent- to turn away from sin

Resurrection- rising again as Jesus did when He came back to life from death

Righteousness- Jesus Christ's perfect obedience transferred to us through His grace

Sacrifice- putting aside one's wants or needs for another

Salvation- being saved from sin and eternal death through grace

Sanctification, sanctify- make holy, our obedient response to Jesus Christ to be more like Him

Saved- set free from the penalty of sin

Scripture- Word of God, the Bible

Sin- disobedience and rebellion against God

Soul- the spiritual nature of humans, thoughts, feelings or emotions

Supplication- asking for humbly or earnestly

Tempt- to test

Trespasses- those things which violate God's will

Trinity- the unfathomable nature of God being three Persons, yet one God

Truth- what God's Word teaches, sometimes Jesus Christ is referred to as the Truth

Worship- to express praise and honor, to adore

Word- God's communication to us, the Bible or sometimes Jesus is referred to as "The Word"

Wrath- God's anger against sin

**I have hidden your word in my heart that
I might not sin against you.
Psalm 119:11**

(but don't hide it so you can't find it again!!)

**Neither do people light a lamp and put it under a
bowl. Instead they put it on its stand, and it gives
light to everyone in the house.
Matthew 5:15**

God... Should I Be Baptized?

1 Corinthians 1:9: "God, who has called you into fellowship with his Son Jesus Christ our Lord, is faithful."

1 John 1:9: "If we confess our sins, he is faithful and just and will forgive us our sins and purify us from all unrighteousness."

Matthew 28:19-20 "Therefore go and make disciples of all nations, baptizing them in the name of the Father and of the Son and of the Holy Spirit, and teaching them to obey everything I have commanded you. And surely I am with you always, to the very end of the age."

Philippians 4:13: "I can do everything through him (Christ) who gives me strength."

Answer Key

Session 1

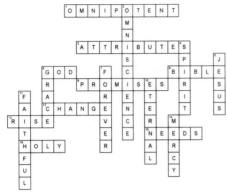

Session 2

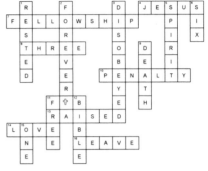

Session 3

Session 4

Puzzle 1- What is God Like?

1. Spirit	4. All Powerful	7. Holy
2. Eternal	5. Knows Everything	8. Always Fair
3. Never Changes	6. Everywhere	9. Faithful
		10. Love

Puzzle 2- Extra! Extra!

A Beautiful Beginning - world, dark, cold, color, creative, God, made, good

Perfect Creation Ruined- man, creation, rule, garden, fruit, tree, disobedience, sin, die, separates

Good News! sin, love, plan, Son, Jesus, confess, forgiveness, good, news

Puzzle 3- Who Should Be Baptized?

THOSE WHO BELIEVE AND RECEIVE

Puzzle 4- Part of the Team!

1. Obey   2. Pray   3. Study His Word   4. Go To Church   5. Tell Others About Jesus
6. Serve Jesus As Lord Of Your Life

God... Should I Be Baptized?

Types of Questions My Pastor May Ask Me
Before I Am Baptized
(possible answers)

1. **Why do you want to be baptized?**
   I want to show everyone that I love God.
   I want to show everyone that I am trusting Christ for salvation.
   I want to follow Jesus and please God.

2. **How do you know that you are going to heaven?**
   I know that I already have everlasting life because Jesus said that if I
   believe Him, trust Him, and obey Him, I will live with Him forever.
   Jesus is in heaven and I will be there when I die, too.

3. **When did Jesus save you?**
   I confessed my sin and repented when I was .....
   Jesus saved me from my sins when I asked Him to forgive my sins and I
   turned from them.

4. **What does baptism mean or show?**
   My baptism will show that I have been washed on the inside.
   My baptism will symbolizes Jesus' death and resurrection.
   My baptism will show that I am part of God's family, the church.

5. **What will happen at your baptism?**
   I will come to church and put on a special robe.
   I will to into the water in the church.
   The Pastor will help me go down into the water and come back up.
   The whole church will sing and pray. Everyone will praise God.

8. **After baptism, what will you do to show that you are on God's team
   and He is Ruler of your life?**
   I will have God's power inside me to help me to obey Him.
   I will pray to God and read my Bible.
   I will come to learn and worship with others at church.
   I will tell others what I am learning about Jesus.

7. **Are you wanting to be baptized to please someone else or is this
   something you really want to do?**
   (Answer from the heart)

What some have said...

"This is a wonderful resource! I have never seen anything like it. As an important act of Christian obedience, baptism should be entered into with understanding and training. This book will help parents, and those who minister to children, not only to examine baptism, but to take advantage of the event of baptism to teach many foundational biblical truths. It accomplishes all of this in ways that are fun and interesting to children."

Dan Pryor
Former U. S. Field Director- Here's Life Inner City
(a ministry of Campus Crusade for Christ)

"Thanks for making 'God.. Should I Be Baptized?' available for our church families. This valuable book helps parents and teachers to transform baptism into a growing spiritual experience. It is a unique, biblically strong resource that becomes a keepsake and a lasting reminder for children wanting to be like Jesus. I looked all over for a tool like this and it's the best."

Mike Akert
Pastor of Children's Ministries
Liberty Bible Church, IN

"I needed an easy to read text which would help me to teach sound doctrine based on God's Word. Your book was just right for us! The lessons in the book were challenging and the concepts were all presented with printed Bible verses, a real time saver... The children are well prepared for their coming baptisms now and they have a personal book to share with family and friends. Thank you for preparing this wonderful study."

Carolyn Trotter
Sunday School Superintendent
Pleasant Valley Baptist Church, CA

"I have used the curriculum for four years and have baptized all of our children using 'God...Should I Be Baptized?' I use the material in a session format, giving the handbooks to the children to take home and work with their parents. The final session is the session in which the baptism takes place. What I like about the material is that it is totally Scriptural. Through the material, the child is taken from a salvation experience and is then discipled into the next step of obedience, water baptism. Moms and dads like it because their children are receiving real training, not just getting 'dunked'. Parents are also included in the training process through checkups and direct help. The format is well done and easy to follow. If a child can read reasonably well, he should be able to complete this material. I feel so strongly about 'God...Should I Be Baptized?' that I have suggested it to my colleagues via e-mail."

Chuck Wasik
Children's Pastor
Racine Assembly of God, WI

God... Should I Be Baptized?

Contributors

Ralph Rittenhouse was on the staff of Campus Crusade for Christ for 13 years, serving in the High School Ministry and then on the National Leadership Team. For the last 28 years Ralph has pastored at Camarillo Community Church in Camarillo, California, a church that is part of the Baptist General Conference. He and his wife, Jackie, have two children and six grandchildren.

Laurie Donahue is the author of *Mr. Blue—a Job for You, The Lord's Supper... Let's Get Ready!, God's Plan... My Response* (LifeSong Publishers), and *A Promise Is...* (Standard Publishing). Laurie directed and choreographed children for the *In My Garden* Videos (Mary Rice Hopkins) and directed, produced and wrote music for *4-Ever His!* She holds a lifetime California Community College Teaching Credential. Laurie lives in Southern California with her husband, Tim, and enjoys 4 grandchildren.

Stanton Ens (page illustrations) spends his time as an engineer and manufacturer of test equipment. Graphic arts and illustration are one of many hobbies, but so far Stanton says he plans to keep his day job. Stanton lives in Camarillo with his wife Kristen, and their two children.

Ed Olson's (cover illustration) illustration and animation career includes projects for the Walt Disney Company, Warner Brothers, Sony and Hanna-Barbera. Believing that the media can be used to reflect Christ in a relevant and respectful way to children, he has developed a design and concept development company which provides production services to Christian-based publishing and media companies. He recently directed and produced an episode of "Adventures in Odyssey" for Focus on the Family. Ed resides in Moorpark, California, with his wife and two children. Visit him at: www.websdirect.com/designloft.

Thank you to many who contributed. Thanks to Pastors, Ralph Rittenhouse, Jim Harmeling, Paul Phillipps, and Paul Ortlinghaus...thanks to Pat Papenhausen, Jane Boyer and Carolyn Trotter for praying, proofing, encouraging and input, to Ed Olson for the cover art, the whole Donahue family for love and support, and especially to our God, for giving the Word.

For Children and Teens from
LifeSong Publishers
More Books by Laurie Donahue

The Lord's Supper...Let's Get Ready!
ISBN 978-09718306-6-0
$10.99 96pp 8.5x11
For children/youth 8-14

Mr. Blue- A Job for You
ISBN 978-09799116-2-0
$15.95 Hardcover 32pp 8x8
For children 3-8
Full color with cut-outs for play

God's Plan... My Response
ISBN 978-09718306-0--8
$9.99 96pp 6x9
For Jr. Hi / Hi School

For Mr. Blue online activity page, go to: www.lifesongpublishers.com/blue

Help Me Remember Series
by Delphine Bates

Help Me Remember
The Days of Creation
ISBN 978-09799116-3-7
$11.95 24pp 8 x 8
for children 3-8

Help Me Remember
The Ten Commandments
ISBN 978-09799116-5-1
$11.95 32pp 8 x 8
for children 3-8

Help Me Remember
The Plagues of Egypt
ISBN 978-09799116-4-4
$11.95 32pp 8 x 8
for children 3-8

"If someone were to ask me right now, 'What did God create on the 5th day?' or 'What's the 5th commandment?' or 'What's the 5th plague brought upon by the Egyptians?'...I would know the answer! And I would have Delphine Bates and her wonderfully imaginative books to thank for it. Honestly, she has given us, young and old alike, an ingenuous way to memorize the Ten Commandments, the Seven Days of Creation and, finally, the Ten Plagues of Egypt. What's more, she makes it so easy. You really must have these little treasures in your home and church library."
—Joni Eareckson Tada, Joni and Friends International Disability Center

Ancient Paths for Modern Women Series
by Judy Gerry

"This is what the Lord says: 'Stand at the crossroads and look; ask for the
ancient paths, ask where the good way is, and walk in it,
and you will find rest for your souls.'" Jeremiah 6:16

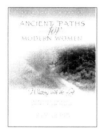   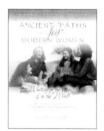

Walking With the Lord
ISBN 978-09718306-2-2
$11.99 100pp 7.5x10

Walking as Wives
ISBN 978-09718306-3-9
$11.99 112pp 7.5x10

Walking as Mothers
and Homemakers
ISBN 978-09718306-4-6
$11.99 110pp 7.5x10

Walking in the Church
and in the World
ISBN 978-09718306-5-3
$11.99 130pp 7.5x10

"Judy Gerry has dug deeply into the sacred records of the Bible to surface divine guidance for women In
every generation. Here is a timely, reassuring and professionally crafted study resource which belongs in
every church library and on the study agenda for thinking women."
Howard G. Hendricks, Distinguished Professor, Dallas Theological Seminary

"Judy... leads women to discover and apply the tried, true, and enduring way laid out for us in the Scripture-
the pathway that leads to blessing and joy. In a day when so many Christian women are floundering and
confused, the wisdom found in this program is timely and desperately needed."
Nancy Leigh DeMoss, Author- Host of Revive Our Hearts Radio

More Books from LifeSong Publishers

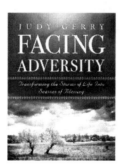 

Facing Adversity Bible Study
by Judy Gerry
ISBN 978-09799116-1-3
$13.99 Softcover 136pp 7.5 x 10

Loving God's Word
by Seth Kniep
ISBN 978-09718306-8-4
$15.99 Softcover 286pp 6 x 9
$20.99 Hardcover

CPSIA information can be obtained at www.ICGtesting.com
Printed in the USA
BVOW01s1817041114

373645BV00002B/6/P